what would you ask?
AMELIA EARHART

Anita Ganeri
Illustrated by Liz Roberts

Thameside Press

Distributed in the United States by
Smart Apple Media
123 South Broad Street
Mankato, Minnesota 56001

Text copyright © Anita Ganeri 1999

Editors: Veronica Ross & Claire Edwards
Designer: Simeen Karim
Illustrator: Liz Roberts
Consultant: Hester Collicutt

Printed in China

ISBN: 1-929298-01-3
Library of Congress Catalog Card Number 99-73398

10 9 8 7 6 5 4 3 2 1

Contents

What do you do?

'I'm an American pilot and explorer.'

In 1928, American pilot Amelia Earhart became the first woman
to fly across the Atlantic Ocean. She made many more
record-breaking flights and became one of the
most famous women in the world.

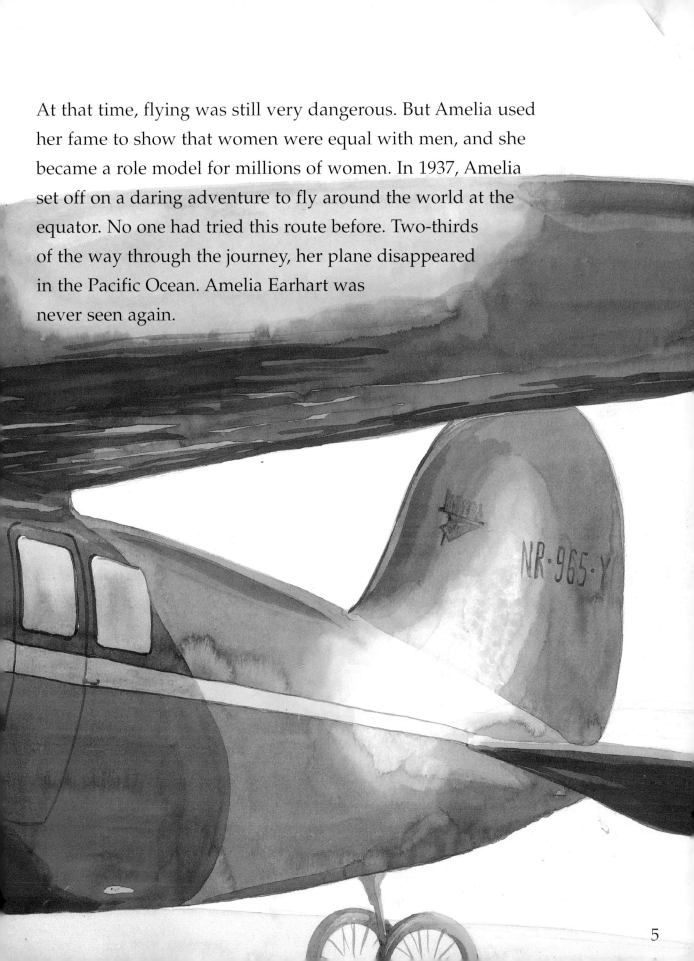

At that time, flying was still very dangerous. But Amelia used her fame to show that women were equal with men, and she became a role model for millions of women. In 1937, Amelia set off on a daring adventure to fly around the world at the equator. No one had tried this route before. Two-thirds of the way through the journey, her plane disappeared in the Pacific Ocean. Amelia Earhart was never seen again.

Where were you born?

"I was born in Atchison, Kansas."

Amelia was born on July 24, 1897 in her grandparents' house in the small town of Atchison, Kansas. She had one sister, Muriel, who was three years younger.

Soon after Amelia was born, her family moved to Kansas City and then to Des Moines in Iowa, where Amelia's father worked as a lawyer. Amelia adored her father, who was kind and loving. But he also liked drinking with his friends, and this finally cost him his job.

Once again the Earharts moved, this time to St. Paul, Minnesota. Money was tight, and the family had to watch every penny they spent. When Mr. Earhart decided to return to Kansas City, Amelia and Muriel moved with their mother to Chicago.

What were you like as a child?

"Kind of a tomboy. I liked doing
things my own way."

Amelia worked hard at school and especially liked science, literature,
and French. But she did not have much to do with the other girls.
She and Muriel spent summer vacations at their grandparents' house.
There were plenty of places to explore, and Amelia's daredevil spirit
often landed her in trouble. She liked to jump over fences instead
of using the gate. She even
hunted rats with a rifle.

One summer, when Amelia was seven years old, her father took her to a fair. Amelia thought that the roller coaster was the most thrilling thing she had ever seen. When she got home, she built her own in the back yard. Her first run on it ended in a crash landing, but Amelia didn't mind. It was just like flying.

Did you always want to be a pilot?

"Not really. But after I visited an airfield,
I just knew I had to fly."

Amelia left high school in 1916, aged 18. In 1917, she spent
Christmas with her sister in Toronto, Canada. World War I
was raging in Europe, and Canada was playing its part. The
hospitals were full of wounded soldiers. Amelia decided at once
to become a Red Cross nurse. For almost a year, she scrubbed
floors, cooked meals, and
gave out medicine in
a military hospital.

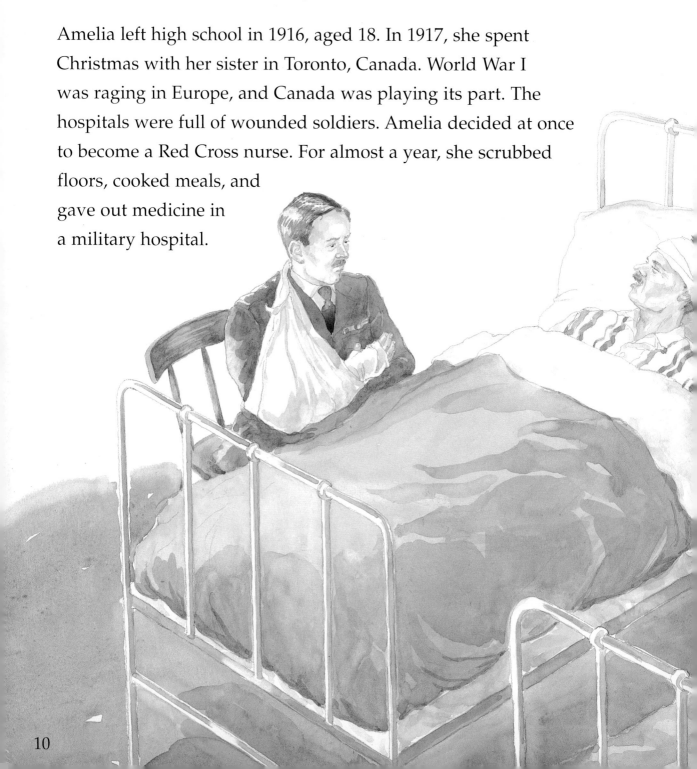

Despite the long hours, Amelia still had fun. Some Canadian pilots invited her to watch an aerobatics show. Suddenly, one of the pilots dove straight at the crowd. Instead of running away in fear, Amelia was thrilled. She knew she just had to fly.

Before long, flying had become the most important thing in Amelia's life. To earn money to pay for flying lessons, Amelia worked as a telephone operator, photographer, truck driver, teacher, and social worker.

How did you learn to fly?

"I asked my father to let me have some flying lessons. He didn't like the idea at first!"

In December 1920, Amelia's father took her to an air show in California where there was a daring display of racing, aerobatics, and wing-walking. The next day, he paid for her first flight ever. Amelia never looked back. Early in 1921, when she was 23, Amelia had her first flying lesson. Her teacher was Neta Snook, one of the very few women pilots. Amelia learned quickly.

Within a few weeks, she took the plane up into the air. Later that year, she made her first solo flight.

Amelia saved up, and a year later, on her 25th birthday, she became the proud owner of her own airplane. She found out all she could about her new plane and how the engine worked. Amelia painted the plane yellow and nicknamed it *The Canary*.

Later that year, she had her first crash and landed in a cabbage patch. After that, she couldn't eat cabbage, but the accident didn't stop her from flying.

Where was your first long flight?

"In 1928, I flew across the Atlantic Ocean."

In 1927, the American pilot Charles Lindbergh had made the first solo flight across the Atlantic in his airplane, the *Spirit of St. Louis*. The following year, Amelia got a phone call from Captain Hilton H. Riley, who had been a pilot in the war. He asked Amelia if she would like to be the first woman to fly the Atlantic.

Amelia accepted eagerly. One morning in June 1928, she joined the seaplane *Friendship*, ready for take-off from Newfoundland in Canada. Amelia's job was to jot down details of their speed, height, and direction.

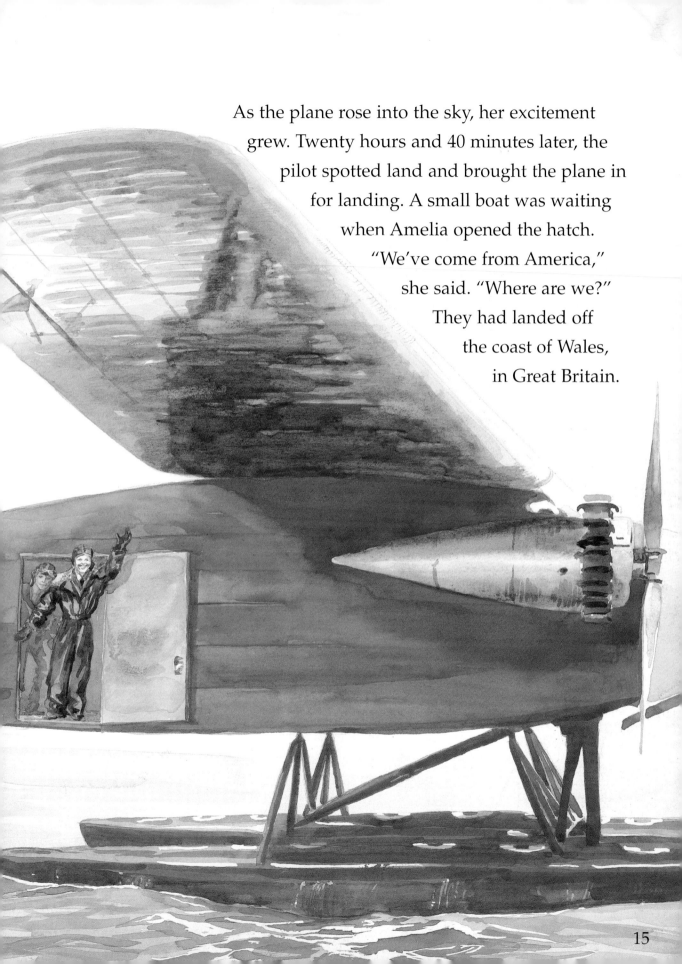

As the plane rose into the sky, her excitement grew. Twenty hours and 40 minutes later, the pilot spotted land and brought the plane in for landing. A small boat was waiting when Amelia opened the hatch. "We've come from America," she said. "Where are we?" They had landed off the coast of Wales, in Great Britain.

15

What was life like after that flight?

"It was very different in lots of ways."

Amelia returned home from her Atlantic flight to find she had become famous. Wherever she went, huge crowds of people flocked to see her. Amelia's name was splashed across all the newspapers. She was known as the First Lady of the Air.

Amelia wrote a book about her flight, called *20 Hours, 40 Minutes*, the time the journey had taken. She gave hundreds of speeches, lectures, and interviews. She used her fame to encourage people to travel on the first passenger aircraft. She often went on the flights herself, talking to passengers and signing autographs. In 1929, Amelia helped set up the Ninety-Nines, a club for women pilots.

In 1931, Amelia married George Putnam, a rich businessman who had organized the Atlantic flight. Now he wanted to make Amelia the most famous woman in America.

What were your other great adventures?

"There were a lot more records to set. I wanted to show people how good women pilots could be."

Despite her fame, Amelia was not content. She still wanted to prove herself as a pilot. In 1930, Amelia flew faster than any woman before. And in 1932, she set out on her greatest adventure yet—to fly solo across the Atlantic.

The journey would be difficult—some said impossible. Amelia took off from Newfoundland and, despite many dangers, landed safely in a field in Ireland. She was the first woman to fly alone across the Atlantic, and she had set a new record of 13 hours and 30 minutes for the journey. She was also the first person to make the crossing twice.

Back home, Amelia was showered with awards. She became friends with kings and presidents, movie stars and explorers. Yet she was always happiest up in the air, away from the crowds.

Were you ever scared?

"Yes, sometimes. But I didn't let that stop me.
I loved flying too much."

In Amelia's time, pilots had to be very brave. Planes
were not built well, and accidents were common. Amelia
had her fair share of crashes. Planes could be brought
down by bad weather or engine failure, and pilots
sometimes lost their way in the dark.

On Amelia's solo flight across the Atlantic, she flew straight into a storm. Ice formed on the plane, causing it to spin. Through the blackness below, she could see the ocean waves. Luckily, as the plane descended, the warmer air melted the ice. Amelia was able to straighten up the plane and hold it level, just in time!

In 1935, Amelia made the first solo flight from Hawaii to California, across the Pacific Ocean. For most of the way, she flew in thick fog. A cover blew off part of the cockpit and freezing air poured into the cabin. When Amelia finally landed, she knew she was lucky to be alive.

What kind of airplane did you fly?

"For my trip around the world, I was given a new plane, called a Lockheed Electra."

In 1936, Amelia began to think about one more long flight. This would be her last, she said. Then she would take life easy. She wanted to fly around the world at the equator, something no one had tried before. For this trip, she needed a new and more powerful plane.

A year earlier, Amelia had taken a position at a university, helping women plan careers in engineering and mechanics. The university set up a fund to buy Amelia the plane of her dreams: a Lockheed Model 10E Electra. It was the sleekest, most modern plane Amelia had ever owned.

The Electra had two engines so it could still fly if one engine failed. It had room for a navigator, since this journey would be too long to fly alone, and so many gadgets that Amelia nicknamed it the *Flying Laboratory*. Amelia practiced flying it every day, especially take-offs and landings.

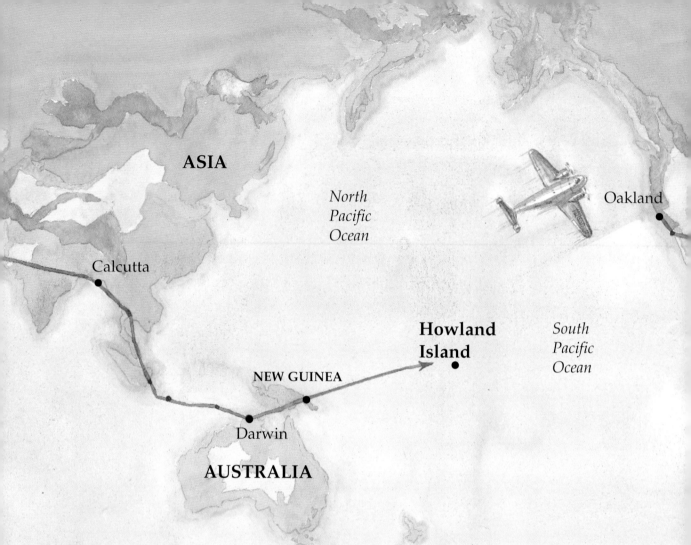

Amelia's last flight

Amelia's flight around the world took a year to plan. After several delays, she and her navigator, a man named Fred Noonan, took off from Oakland, California on May 20, 1937. For a month, they flew eastward, along the coast of South America, across the Atlantic to Africa and Asia, then to the island of New Guinea. They crossed jungles, seas, deserts, and mountains.

The most dangerous part of the journey was still to come, though. Amelia had to fly from New Guinea to Howland Island, a tiny speck of land in the middle of the Pacific Ocean. It was extremely tricky to find. Early on July 2, Amelia steered the Electra down the runway and into the air.

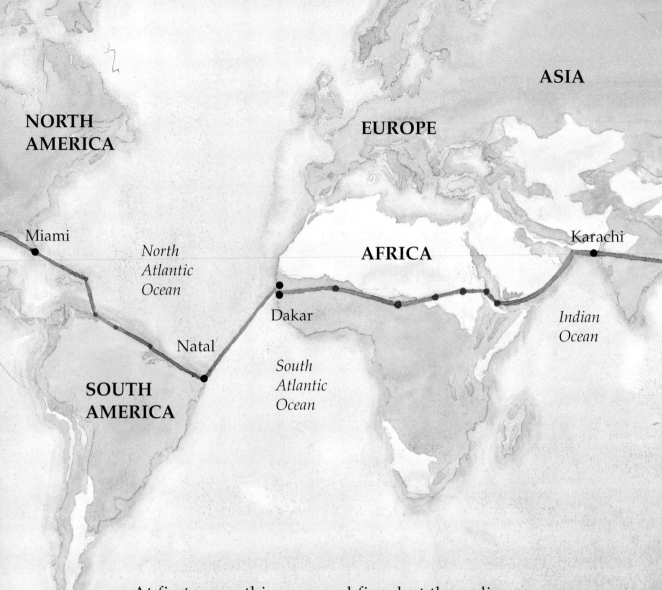

NORTH
AMERICA

ASIA

EUROPE

Miami

Karachi

*North
Atlantic
Ocean*

AFRICA

Dakar

Natal

*Indian
Ocean*

SOUTH
AMERICA

*South
Atlantic
Ocean*

At first, everything seemed fine, but the radio messages
from Amelia soon got fainter. The last call came the following
morning. Fuel was running low, Amelia said, and they could not see land.
Then the radio went dead. The plane never reached the island. Despite a
huge search, no trace of Amelia, Noonan, or the Electra was ever found.

Amelia Earhart was just 39 years old when she died. But in her short
life, she inspired millions of people all over the world. Through her
kindness, courage, and determination, she showed everyone, especially
women, that dreams can come true.

The Lockheed Electra

The Lockheed Electra 10E was the plane flown by Amelia on her last flight around the world.

The 10E Electra had a wingspan of 56 feet. Its body was 38 feet long and ten feet high.

The 10E Electra was the first all-metal passenger aircraft. It had two engines and was the only plane large enough and strong enough to carry the fuel needed for Amelia's long flight.

Only 15 10E Electras were made by the Lockheed company in the U.S.A. The first was made in 1934.

Empty, the 10E Electra weighed 6,447 pounds. With its crew and heavy fuel load, this increased to 15,685 pounds.

The 10E's maximum speed was 200 miles per hour.

At maximum speed, the 10E Electra could fly from New York to California in about $13\frac{1}{2}$ hours. Today's newest plane, the Boeing 777, would take just four hours to complete the journey.

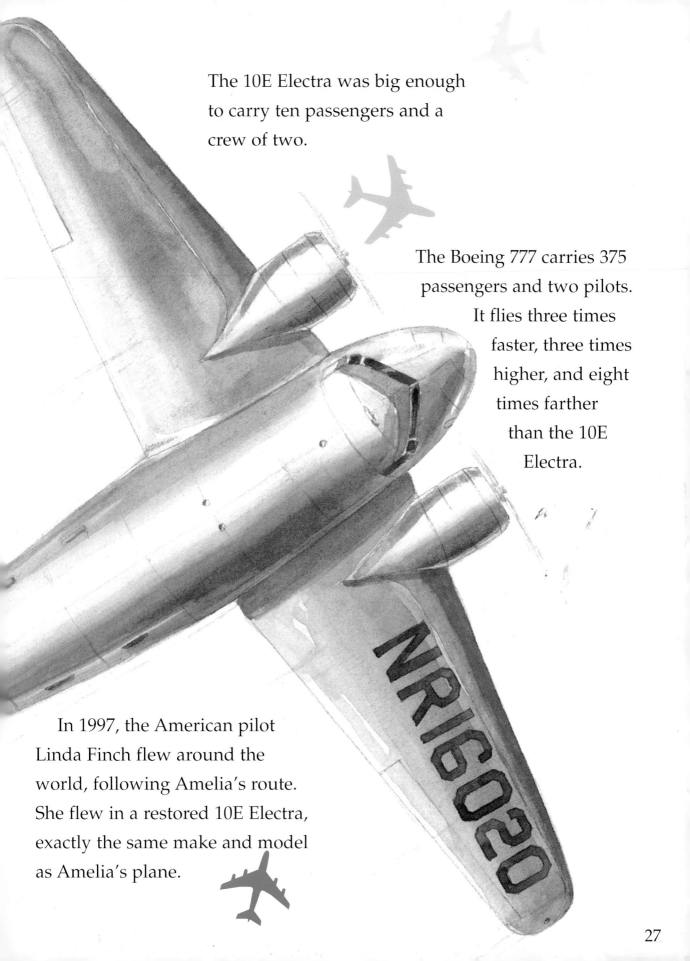

The 10E Electra was big enough to carry ten passengers and a crew of two.

The Boeing 777 carries 375 passengers and two pilots. It flies three times faster, three times higher, and eight times farther than the 10E Electra.

In 1997, the American pilot Linda Finch flew around the world, following Amelia's route. She flew in a restored 10E Electra, exactly the same make and model as Amelia's plane.

Some important dates

1897 Amelia Earhart is born in Atchison, Kansas, on July 24.

1903 The Wright brothers make the first powered flight.

1916 Amelia graduates from high school in Chicago.

1917 Amelia works as a Red Cross nurse in a military hospital in Toronto, Canada.

1919 Amelia becomes a student at Columbia University.

1920 Amelia takes her first flight, as a passenger.

1921 Amelia starts to take flying lessons from Neta Snook, one of the very few women pilots. Later that year, Amelia makes her first solo flight.

1922 Amelia buys her first airplane, nicknamed *The Canary*.

1923 Amelia receives her pilot's license. She was only the sixteenth woman in the world to have one.

1925-8 Amelia works as a teacher, then a social worker, in Boston.

1928 Amelia becomes the first woman to fly across the Atlantic Ocean. She is part of a three-person crew aboard the seaplane *Friendship*. Amelia's book, *20 Hours, 40 Minutes*, is published.

1929 Amelia flies in the first ever Women's Air Derby and finishes third. She also helps to found the Ninety-Nines, an international club for women pilots.

1930 Amelia flies faster than any woman before, at 180 miles per hour.

1931 Amelia marries George Putnam, a wealthy publisher and businessman.

1932 Amelia becomes the first woman to fly across the Atlantic Ocean solo. She receives the gold medal from the National Geographic Society and the Distinguished Flying Cross.

1935 Amelia makes the first solo flight from Hawaii to California. She also becomes the first person to fly nonstop from Mexico City to Newark, New Jersey. She joins Purdue University to advise women on careers in engineering and mechanics.

1937 Amelia sets out to fly around the world at the equator.

1937 On July 3, Amelia's plane disappears in the Pacific Ocean before she reaches Howland Island.

1964 An American pilot, Joan Merriam Smith, finally becomes the first woman to fly around the world, following Amelia's route. This route becomes known as the Earhart Trail.

1997 Linda Finch flies around the world, following Amelia's route, in a restored 10E Electra.

Glossary

aerobatics Performing daring aerial stunts, such as looping the loop, or diving low, for fun or to entertain people.

cockpit The part of an airplane where the pilot and crew sit and fly the plane.

daredevil A person who acts without any thought of danger.

equator An imaginary line around the middle of the earth. Amelia's route around the equator was 28,570 miles long.

Charles Lindbergh (1902–1974) An American pilot who made the first nonstop solo flight across the Atlantic in 1927. He flew from New York to Paris in 33 hours and 30 minutes.

military To do with the armed forces (the army, navy, or air force).

navigator The person who works out the route that a plane follows on a flight. He or she uses maps and instruments to make sure that the plane keeps to that route.

nickname Another name for something or someone. Nicknames are often funny or affectionate.

Ninety-Nines (99s) The club Amelia Earhart helped set up in 1929 to encourage women pilots. It was called the 99s because it originally had 99 members. Today, it is still active, with 70,000 members all over the world.

passenger aircraft An airplane that carries passengers.

pilot's license The license given to people who have passed their flying test. They also have to spend many hours in the air, sometimes flying solo.

Red Cross An international health care organization. It was set up in 1863 by a Swiss man who had seen the terrible suffering caused by war. There are now branches of the society in over one hundred countries.

restore To restore means to bring back. Restoring an old plane, for example, means to bring it back to flying condition.

role model A role model is someone you admire and look up to because of their personality or achievements.

seaplane An airplane designed to take off from and land in water.

solo On your own. Flying solo means that you fly on your own, acting as pilot and navigator.

wingspan The distance from the tip of one wing to the tip of the other wing.

wing-walking A brave stunt performed at air shows, when one person stands on the plane's wing as the plane flies.

World War I In 1914 war broke out between the Allies (Britain, France, Russia, and, in 1917, the U.S.A.) and the Central Powers (Germany, Turkey, and Austria-Hungary). Countries in the British Empire, including Canada, also fought. The Allies won the war. By the time the war ended in 1918, 10 million soldiers had been killed in battle.

Wright brothers Two American brothers, Orville (1871–1948) and Wilbur (1867–1912) Wright, who made the first powered flight on December 17, 1903.

Index